Hometown

Tehya Russell

BookLeaf
Publishing

India | USA | UK

Presentation by *BookLeaf Publishing*

Web: www.bookleafpub.com

E-mail: info@bookleafpub.com

ISBN: 9789358369687

First edition 2023

For small towns and the people that choose
to love them.

ACKNOWLEDGEMENT

I'd like to thank the publishers and editors at BookLeaf Publishing for taking the time to work with me on this project. I'd also like to take a moment to thank the friends, teachers, family members, and others who helped me get here.

Hometown

A dusty little town
North of nowhere
With a single main road,
Bleached and broken
From years of abuse
By log trucks and pickups,
Potholes dotting cement
Like freckles,
So torn up
It looks more like
A crumpled piece of paper
Than a road with
A single destination.

Chapters

Sometimes I can feel the story end
Before it even starts.
It seems like every chapter
Is written by broken hearts.

What We Miss

I wonder how much of life
Is lived in the things
We don't do.
How much it breathes
In the spaces between words.
How it hangs in the air,
Between us,
In the moments that pass us by.

All Year Round

The air here smells like
Fresh cut grass,
Like wildfire smoke,
Like cigarettes
And stale beer
And fireworks,
Like engines in old trucks
And melting ice cream
And the earth after it rains.
The air here smells like
Summer, all year round.

To the Moon

My greatest fear
Is that one day
You'll stop loving me
And I'll never figure out
How to stop loving you.

The sun will set and rise.
The stars will change
With the seasons.
And I'll still be here,
Whispering your name
To the moon.

The People Here

The people here are strong and hard to get rid of.
They sweat the day in hard labor
And come home to families at night.
They sit around broken tables,
Eat TV dinners on the couch.
Their children tell them of big dreams.
They do not tell the kids
They used to dream too.
They smile and say things like
"Get good grades"
Or "go check on your sister"
Or "did you do your chores?"
They do not tell them
That this is a place that no one ever leaves.

H.O.M.E.

Heavy is the heart that
Only knows how to love when
Memories are all they have left of
Everyone that loved them.

After It Ends

There's a good chance
That neither of us will make it out of this
Quite the way we went into it.
A chance that your name will be another scar
On my wrist
In my memories
For more time to come
Than ever we spent together.
There's a good chance
That you'll forget something in my room
The day you come to grab the rest.
And it will sit in my windowsill
Collecting dust
Until one day I look at it
And I won't see it at all.
I think that's how healing goes.
Like forgetting.
Slowly fading away until it doesn't hurt
Then suddenly you don't think of it at all.
Will you remember my name?
Will I remember yours?
Like I said, it's on my wrist now.
But I never remember half the tattoos on my
body anyways.

Wildfires

Year after year,
The heat creeps in
And the summers get dryer
And the wildfires
Dance around the woods,
Flame tongues licking at treetops,
Stopping just before
A house
A store
Maybe even more.
This town breathes smoke
But it does not burn.

Blank Page

I found myself in books,
In the way a writer might see me.
I'm a character
Waiting for redemption,
A love interest,
A happy ending.

In books,
I live in castles,
In dorm rooms,
In a cottage,
In a little place above a cafe.

In books,
I'm holding a sword,
Acing big tests,
Wearing silk gowns,
Baking muffins,
Falling in love.

In life,
I sit by a cafe window,
Staring at a blank page,
Not quite ready
To write myself in.

The Thing About Hearts

I have so many stories
With people I no longer know.
The friendship fades,
The memories stay,
And sometimes I'm reminded
Of who we were
Before it fell apart.
That's the thing about hearts-
They hold on just a little too tight,
Even if the people don't.

H.E.A.R.T.

How do you stop bleeding on
Everyone who never cut you
And when are you
Ready
To heal?

The People Here II

The people here
Grow dandelions in their yards
And the whole town
Looks like wishes and sunshine.

Phone Call

In a perfect world,
You call to tell me about your day
And I listen.
I laugh and nod at all the right parts,
And I forget that you can't see it.
You talk so fast because you're excited,
And when you pause to catch your breath,
The phone makes a small crinkle sound,
And I know it's you smiling.
And I promise that I'm smiling too,
Even as I'm missing you.

I am the book.

One side of my skin bleeds
And the other side bruises,
Poems leaking from my fingertips
Like ink from a broken bottle,

Mark the page
Mark my skin
Mark my words

A book with a leather bound cover
Carefully stitched together
And still falling apart,

Heart on the sleeve.

My Own Ghost

And here I am again,
Haunting the places I used to love,
Looking for traces of my own ghost.
Is she in the mirrors? In the walls?
She calls to me still.
I don't know when she and I
Became different things,
And I haven't found her since.
Parts of her had to die
So parts of me could exist.

Part of me is still a kid.

Part of me
Is still a kid,
Running around
With muddy feet
And sticky ice cream fingers,
Picking dandelions
To buy wishes,
Chasing minnows
In the river,
Thinking shooting stars
Are fallen angels.

Swingset

There's something different about the way
The swings hang still
Now that you're older.
They don't just sit there, waiting.
It's not just an open spot for you anymore.
It's an empty park and empty playground
And it's cold at night
And you swear the swing looks lonely.
Maybe the wind whistles softly as it weaves through
The chains that used to hold you up and lift you high.
There's something sad about how
Lonely the park is
Now that you're alone.

You feel like sunshine.

You feel like sunshine-
Bright, warm.
A smile that looks like hope
And a voice that sounds like a hug.
You're the color yellow-
The color of honey
And wildflowers.
You're the kind of person
That can make broken people
Believe in love.

Cleaning Your Room

The thing about cleaning your room
Is that you have to get off your ass and start.
You have to choose
What corner to do first,
What gets thrown away,
Which clothes get folded
And which get rewashed.
Sometimes you find something
You'd forgotten you'd ever had.
Like a trophy from middle school,
Or an old favorite t-shirt,
Or a picture of that old best friend
You don't talk to anymore.
And you'll stop cleaning,
Just for a moment.
Just long enough to let your mind wander.
And suddenly you're drowning.
But now you're not just drowning
In dirty laundry
And snack wrappers
And receipts you forgot to throw away.
Now you're drowning
In memories.
And one always leads to another.
And you sit there and wonder

"How long has it been since I wore this last?"
Or
"I can't remember why we stopped talking"
Or maybe
"When did I stop doing things I used to love?"
And
"When did I start to become a completely
different person?"
Maybe there isn't an answer.
Maybe you look for one
A little too long
And it still doesn't come.
But then you'll look around
And remember
That you are cleaning your room.
And you'll set old things aside
And keep going.
Maybe your mind stays stuck
On memories while you work.
Maybe the cleaning is slower now
Than when you started.
Maybe it's not.
But you're cleaning your room,
And eventually it will be
Like it was before you neglected it.
Today.
Tomorrow.
Eventually.
And I think maybe healing

Is like cleaning your room.
You have to decide to start
And to keep going.
And maybe it doesn't get done
All in one day.
But you're doing it.
One load of laundry,
One hard memory,
At a time.

Graffiti

Do you ever look at graffiti
And wonder where that person is now?

How far away were they
When they spray painted the train cars?
Cities? States?
How much of the world
Has their mark already seen?

And is the couple still together?
The one that carved their initials
In a heart
On the park picnic table?
And do either of them still come
To sit there in the summer
If they broke up?

Do you ever look at graffiti
And wonder
What it is that fascinates people
About forever?